THE BEST OF FRIENDS

For Michael
and
In Memory of My Father

HUGH WHITEMORE

The Best of friends

adapted from
the letters and writings of
Dame Laurentia McLachlan, Sir Sydney Cockerell
and George Bernard Shaw

AMBER LANE PRESS

First published in 1988 by
Amber Lane Press Ltd.
9 Middle Way
Oxford OX2 7LH

Typeset in Ehrhardt by Oxford Computer Typesetting

Printed and manufactured in Great Britain by
Cotswold Press Ltd., Eynsham, Oxford

ISBN: 0 906399 86 6

INTRODUCTION

Sometime in 1976, Michael Redington, whom I had met when he was a programme executive with an Independent Television company, enquired whether I would consider writing a TV script based on the friendship between Bernard Shaw and Dame Laurentia McLachlan, one-time Abbess of Stanbrook Abbey in Worcestershire. He gave me a book about Dame Laurentia, *In a Great Tradition*, and photo-copies of some of the letters she and GBS had written to each other. I found the material interesting and, under commission from London Weekend Television, I wrote a draft script. Although Redington and the TV people were pleased with my work, the programme was never made and the project disappeared into oblivion. Or so I thought. But a few years later, in 1980, I was again approached by Redington — who is, I was soon to discover, a man of dogged tenacity. By this time, he had returned to his first love, the theatre; and he asked me to look again at the Shaw/Dame Laurentia material and to see if it might work on the stage. I agreed to do so. It was then that I began to investigate the man who had introduced GBS to the nun: Sir Sydney Cockerell, an inveterate letter-writer and diarist, who had been Director of the Fitzwilliam Museum in Cambridge. Cockerell's characteristics — prickly, pedantic, a collector of gossip and famous people, a man who pursued friendship with tireless energy — made him an attractive subject for a dramatist to explore. Quite clearly, the play — if there was to be one — should involve not just Shaw and Dame Laurentia, but Cockerell as well.

About this time, James Roose-Evans appeared on the scene. He was working (as adaptor and director) on the stage version of *84 Charing Cross Road*, which Michael Redington was to produce with great success in the West End; he also had a close association with the community at Stanbrook. Furthermore, he had been on the staff of the Royal Academy of Dramatic Art when I had been a hopeful (but woefully untalented) pupil. He was extremely enthusiastic about the project, and it was agreed that he should direct the play. The trouble was, no play existed. I had become deeply involved with writing something else (*Pack of Lies*, which Reding-ton subsequently produced) and the months slipped by. I did, however, make contact with one of Cockerell's most notable friends, Sir Alec Guinness. In replying to my initial letter, he wrote:

> I am rather astonished at what appears to be a revival of interest in Sir Sydney Cockerell — in American academic circles this appears to be very much so — but am delighted to hear about your play, and wish you great success with the production. I first met Sydney in the early sping of 1939 when he was a guest at the Chester Beattys' house — well, palace — outside Cairo. My wife and I were taken to tea there by a charming couple who said, while on our way, "The trouble is they have a cantankerous old man called Cockerell staying and we advise you to avoid him." Well, I didn't find him in the least cantankerous. I saw him a few times after that and then the war years intervened. I learned a lot from him; he was always quick to point out any solecisms. And I cherished his tales of William Morris, Hardy, Tolstoy and T.E. Lawrence.

Pack of Lies was produced in London in October 1983, and once again I tried to get going on *The Best of Friends* — I had found a title for it, if nothing else. But an interesting film job came along, and then, having read Andrew Hodges' remarkable biography, I was eager to write a play about the mathematician Alan Turing; I persuaded Redington that the Cockerell project should wait until I had written this new play. This proved to be a long and arduous task, and it was three years before *Breaking the Code* reached the London stage. During this time, everyone concerned began to have serious doubts as to whether I would ever actually write a play about Shaw, Cockerell and Dame Laurentia. In a letter to the nuns of Stanbrook, Michael Redington wrote:

> James Roose-Evans telephoned me late last night to say he had seen you yesterday afternoon and that you had expressed your concern and disappointment in the lack of progress regarding the play — and indeed, not hearing news of any developments.

The fault was entirely mine. But then, early in 1987, everything seemed to fall into place and I wrote a first draft. Armed with these preliminary pages, Roose-Evans and I went to Stanbrook Abbey to examine their collection of Dame Laurentia/Cockerell letters — hundreds and hundreds of them — which we read with growing excitement and delight. I hurried back to London, and the final version of the play at last began to take shape.

As always, I owe a great deal to those friends who have read the dizzying succession of drafts, and who have given me their encouragement and advice. Most particularly, I should like to thank Dame Felicitas Corrigan of Stanbrook Abbey, whose perceptive suggestions have enriched the play significantly. I have dedicated this published text to Michael Redington; it was his idea, after all — and I only hope his patience will be happily rewarded.

This text went to the printers in January 1988 and, therefore, it does not include revisions made during rehearsals.

Hugh Whitemore

The Best of Friends was first presented by Michael Redington at the Apollo Theatre, London, on 10th February, 1988, with the following cast:

SCC:..John Gielgud
GBS:..Ray McAnally
DLM:.. Rosemary Harris

Director: James Roose-Evans
Designer: Julia Trevelyan Oman
Lighting: Mick Hughes
Sound: Peter Still

The sitting room and conservatory of 21 Kew Gardens Road, which reminded one visitor of "a rather down-at-heel vicarage". An old man with a trim Vandyke beard sits dozing on a Morris chair, a natural-coloured Arab straight-cut long coat covering his everyday suit. This is Sydney Carlyle Cockerell, referred to in the play-text as SCC. Bundles of papers and letters are stacked neatly on a large tray at his side. Nearby stands a book-case filled with exquisitely bound volumes; photographs of close friends (including Shaw and Dame Laurentia) are clustered on the shelves. Faded, peeling wallpaper. Framed drawings by Rossetti, Burne-Jones and Ruskin. Beside the bed is a table and telephone.

On the left is a writing desk, surrounded by many books. Here sits a familiar figure with a fine white beard: Bernard Shaw — GBS. On the right, French windows open onto the conservatory, where a Benedictine nun is sitting: Dame Laurentia McLachlan — DLM. The bars of the French windows discreetly suggest the grille through which she spoke to visitors at Stanbrook Abbey.

In 1924, when Dame Laurentia and Shaw first met, she was 58, GBS was 68 and SCC was 57. Although bed-ridden for the last years of his life, dramatic licence should allow SCC to move freely around the stage. Sometimes the three friends address each other directly; sometimes they soliloquise or speak to the audience, moving unobtrusively from one mode to another.

ACT ONE

Dawn in Kew, Worcestershire and Ayot St Lawrence. SCC is dozing. GBS is at his desk, working. DLM stands at an open door, looking out into a cloister garden. A cuckoo is echoing in the valley. GBS looks up: he also hears it. SCC, stirring, hears it too. The Abbey clock strikes 5.00. SCC checks the time and winds his watch. GBS exits for an early morning stroll. A bell tolls to awaken the community at Stanbrook. DLM hurries off. SCC gathers together his papers, examining them with a magnifying glass.

SCC: Fifty-eight years ago I went to Russia to visit Tolstoy. It was excessively hot, I remember. July 13th, 1903. He lived near the village of Yasnaya Polyana. The prospect on either side of the road was very beautiful: great sweeps of unenclosed cornland and woods chiefly of close-set birches, far taller than any I have seen in England: long hills: wide strips of roadside pasture, very flowery, with blue cranesbill, larkspur, dog-daisies and willow herb. [*Brief pause.*] The amazing thing is, I am now twenty years older than Tolstoy was then. I can't believe that. He seemed as old as God, however old that's supposed to be. And I am now twenty years older. More dead than alive, I often think. Sometimes in the middle of the night, I feel so weak that a puff of wind would blow me out like a candle. I shan't live through another winter. [*Brief pause.*] Tolstoy gave us an excellent lunch: barley-broth, veal and salad. Crimean wine. Very good. We talked of Dickens, William Morris and Ruskin. He admired them all greatly. After lunch, he took me upstairs to the billiard room. It was quite extraordinary. The table was piled high with thousands of unopened letters from all parts of the world. I stared in amazement; Tolstoy merely shrugged. Later he showed me his work-room: very simply furnished, without a carpet. Then we returned to the verandah and drank a farewell cup of tea. One had only to meet Tolstoy to feel that he lived on a different plane from most people: a plane in which love of family and love of country are entirely merged in love of man and love of God — though what God is or whether there be one God or more than one, he told me he did not know. That, I suppose, is why Dame Laurentia regarded him with some suspicion. I think she was fearful that Tolstoy's work might be inconsistent with her course of life. I did my best to reassure her. Dame Laurentia McLachlan of Stanbrook Abbey: one of my dearest and closest friends.

[GBS *enters and shakes the rain from his clothes.*]

GBS: The road that led us to Stanbrook Abbey was little more than an oozy quagmire of liquid gamboge. It was raining heavily. I'd gone there because Sydney Cockerell had urged me to do so. He was then Director of the Fitzwilliam Museum in Cambridge, and had a wide circle of friends with whom he corresponded very regularly.

SCC: [*climbing out of bed*] I like people of various kinds and keep my friends in different boxes. What I chiefly demand in them is understanding and character — if they also have looks and wit and morals of some kind, however unconventional, so much the better. Some friends I have to keep apart; others I wish to bring together. I told Dame Laurentia. . .

[DLM *enters.*]

. . . that I had known Bernard Shaw for many years and regarded him not only as one of the cleverest but as one of the best and honestest of living Englishmen.

GBS: We were shown into a small, bare room: the parlour. The community at Stanbrook is enclosed and Dame Laurentia was shielded from us by an iron grille. It was an odd experience; I had never talked through bars before. But Charlotte and I like her *very* much.

DLM: Mr and Mrs Shaw came to see me yesterday afternoon. They were charming. We discussed his play, *St Joan*, with other subjects, in a very pleasant conversation. I was greatly interested to meet such a famous man, and my impression was that we got on very well together.

SCC: I told Ouida about my trip to Russia. Her response was most surprising. Ouida had once been a fashionable novelist, but when I knew her she was old and poor and lived in a fisherman's cottage in Tuscany. She thought Tolstoy was absolutely silly. "He has no judgement of literature," she said, "and not much of men." She seemed to think he would've been a far greater man if he hadn't been born a Russian. I can't imagine why this was. She had some very curious ideas. When we first met, she was unable to believe that I was merely Sydney Carlyle Cockerell. She was convinced that I must be a distinguished personage in disguise.

GBS: [*addressing* SCC] Why is she called Dame?

SCC: Why is who called what?

GBS: Dame! — Dame! — why is she called Dame?

SCC: There's no need to shout.

GBS: You're going deaf.

SCC: Nonsense. What did you say?

GBS: I was asking about your friend, the nun: why is she called Dame?

SCC: It's just a form of address, that's all.

GBS: Like monks calling themselves Dom.

SCC: Exactly. Shall you go to see her again?

GBS: No, never. [*Briefest pause.*] How long has she been there?

SCC: Almost fifty years.

GBS: Oh well, that alters the case entirely. I'll go whenever I can.
        [SCC *laughs.*]

SCC: My father once said to me, "When you grow up, I expect you to be a better man than I am." Though I was only ten when he died, I was old enough to realise the impossibility of this. However successful I may have been as a Museum official, I am in most respects a quite insignificant person. Strip off the veneer of distinguished men and women from whose friendship or acquaintance I have gained an unfair lustre, and what remains? I haven't a spark of imagination; and sometimes I look despairingly at my useless hands that have never been taught to fashion the smallest thing. Perhaps this is why I have always tried to be with people better than myself — and never did a man have such a galaxy of kind and dear friends. Perhaps that's why I go on enjoying life to such a preposterous degree.

[SCC *returns to his papers.*]

DLM: I am now in possession of my own copy of *St Joan*, adorned with the inscription "To Sister Laurentia from Brother Bernard". [*The book is in her hand.*] Mr Shaw is becoming quite monastic. *St Joan* is a wonderful play, reaching in its simplicity (which must have cost much labour) a high degree of art. Joan herself is beautifully portrayed, although Mr Shaw's version of the trial does not please me: he is far too sympathetic to the Protestants.

[GBS *swings round, with* DLM's *letter in his hand.*]

GBS: My dear Sister Laurentia, In reading heathen literature like mine, you must remember that I am addressing an audience not exclusively Catholic, including not only Protestants but also Indians and Orientals. If I wrote from an exclusively Catholic point of view my book would reach no further than the penny lives of the saints which they sell in the Churches of Ireland. I want my sound to go out into all lands!

SCC: Shaw once told me that he always composed in shorthand; the text was then typewritten by his secretary.

GBS: I let the play write itself and shape itself. Sometimes I do not see what the play is driving at until quite a long time after I have finished it.

SCC: What about the plot? How do you think of that?

GBS: I never invent a plot. Quite often I don't know what's going to happen on the next page. Plot has always been the curse of serious drama, and indeed of serious literature of any kind.

SCC: How extraordinary.

GBS: Extraordinary . . . ?

SCC: You make it sound so easy.

GBS: And so it is. When people ask me whether it is difficult to write plays, I always reply that it is either easy or impossible. It may be laborious: that is quite another matter; but unless the novice can do it from the first without any serious trouble or uncertainty he had better not do it at all: it is not his job.

DLM: Dear Mr Cockerell, Last Friday I had another visit from Brother Bernard and Mrs Shaw. He looks amazingly young and fresh, with the blue eyes of a child, and I do like him. He has such a pretty knack of turning on you with a whimsical smile when you think you have caught him. He invited me to take a drive, but as I had not your permission, I refused! I think it is wonderfully nice of them to come to see the likes o' me. Unfortunately we had only a quarter of an hour together as it was nearly time for our Vespers.

GBS: [*opening a letter*] I have been awarded the Nobel Prize for Literature, which I assume is a token of gratitude for a sense of world relief that I have published nothing this year. I refused the prize — £7000 — saying that the money was a lifebelt thrown to a swimmer who has already reached the shore in safety.

[*SCC hears this, sharing his amusement with* DLM.]

My decision has had an alarming effect on hundreds of people, especially Americans, who have written to suggest that since I am so wealthy I should lend them something. Thus I am now practising a complicated facial expression which combines universal benevolence with a savage determination not to save any American from ruin by a remittance of $500. [*The letter he is reading is clearly another request for money.*] I can forgive Alfred Nobel for having invented dynamite — but only a fiend in human form could have invented the Nobel Prize!

[*SCC laughs and then concentrates on writing a letter.*]

DLM: Brother Bernard has given me a copy of *The Apple Cart*, which I read with great delight. What dialogue! Act II interested me very much; under that cold-and-clear-as-ice-brain I find a good deal of emotion.

SCC: [*glances up briefly*] I am not aware of any emotional episodes in Brother Bernard's life, and I should have supposed that he never had an entanglement from which he could not retreat at will.

GBS: I found sex hopeless as a basis for permanent relations, and never dreamt of marriage in connection with it. I put everything else before it, and never refused or broke an engagement to speak on Socialism to pass a gallant evening. I liked sexual intercourse because of its amazing power of producing a celestial flood of emotion and exaltation of existence which, however momentary, gave me a sample of what may one day be the normal state of being for mankind in intellectual ecstasy.

SCC: Like Bernard Shaw I did not kiss a woman until I was twenty-eight — and then she kissed me first! Since then I have been on kissing and caressing terms with very many women, but I have only had the final intimacy with one of them, my wife, whom I married when I was forty; before that, poverty protected me from matrimony. As is happens, I was strongly sexed and my chastity was severely tried; but I have never been able to make up my mind whether my abstention was prompted by honourable scruples or by fear of the possible consequences.

GBS: At one time I thought that the only sensible way of finding a wife was to advertise for one. "Wanted: a reasonably healthy woman of about sixty, accustomed to plain vegetarian cooking, and able to read and write enough to forward letters when her husband is away, but otherwise uneducated. Must be plain featured, and of an easy, unjealous temperament. No relatives if possible. Must not be a lady. One who has never been in a theatre preferred."

DLM: A nun ought to be a brave person, not just a nice little thing. We have been called out of the world to work for God, to bear things for Him, to endure what He pleases to inflict on us in the way of trials, spiritual or otherwise; and, of course, to pray for those we have left behind and for all in general. We may have tried not to hear the call, to silence it even, but the gentle voice has persisted in its appeal, and here we are. We all know the joy and pain of that mysterious call. *Providebam Dominum in conspectu meo semper* — I set the Lord always in my sight. To my mind, people make the spiritual life far too complicated. There should be no problems. Simply steep yourself in God.

SCC: Dear Sister Laurentia, I am a man without any set creed — too much in sympathy with all great religions to adhere exclusively to one, too much in awe of the great mysteries to accept any solution of them. I have been to Assisi for love of St Francis and have looked at Damascus with more reverence for the sake of St Paul. But I should look with similar feelings on places associated with Buddha and Confucius — and having seen a little of Mahommedans and known the late Grand Mufti of Egypt, who was one of the wisest, gentlest and most venerable of men, I am opposed to their being converted into Christians or into anything other than more enlightened Mahommedans. The worst of believing in any one religion is that it leads one to regard all other religions as wrong — I prefer to think that there is an element of truth, larger or smaller, in them all. It is my belief that the three greatest men the world has produced are Jesus, Michelangelo and Alexander the Great — *in that order.* I tell you all this that you may realise what manner of infidel you are dealing with.

DLM: It is very nice of you to tell me your religious views so frankly. You won't mind my saying that I think a man without a set creed is very much to be pitied.

> [DLM *has been reading* SCC*'s letter; now she puts it away and starts tidying her desk.*]

While acknowledging all the good there is in the different ways men have of expressing their religion, one cannot see how all can be equally right — especially if we grant (as you perhaps do not grant) that God has made a definite revelation to men. I am not going to believe that you are a plain infidel, but I do not see where God and Christianity come into your system. Of course we do not advocate indiscriminate proselytising, but I do believe that St Francis, after he had converted *you*, would have gone off to Egypt to try to make a Christian of your late friend, the Grand Mufti!

SCC: I am relieved to find you no more shocked by my unbeliefs than I am shocked by your beliefs. Of course we are both bound to be a little shocked and to wish it were otherwise, but there seems to be nothing to prevent our being as good friends as ever.

[GBS *speaks to* DLM.]

GBS: You'll be surprised — and, I hope, delighted — to know that I am about to become a pilgrim.

DLM: What sort of pilgrim?

GBS: I'm going on a trip to the Holy Land: Jerusalem, Nazareth, Bethlehem, Damascus.

DLM: You must take me with you.

GBS: I wish I could.

DLM: In spirit. You must let my spirit run about the Holy places I have never seen but seem to know so well.

GBS: I certainly will.

DLM: And please lay my love and reverence at Our Lord's feet; bring me back some little memento from Calvary.

GBS: Yes, I will.

DLM: When do you leave?

GBS: March.

[*He moves to the door, picking up a straw hat.*]

We go by way of Marseilles and Egypt.

[GBS *exits.*]

SCC: [*reading from his diary*] In the 1890's I went to Italy with Shaw. The trip was organised for the Art Workers' Guild, and there were about thirty of us — all men. During the course of my life I have made eighty-four trips abroad, travelling most frequently to Beauvais and Chartres — or

"Charters" as Ruskin used to call it. My wife, being an invalid, never came with me. GBS was not very enthusiastic about Venice: St Mark's, he thought, would make an ideal railway station. I suffered badly from mosquito bites and fleas. Shaw said that the only remedy was to perspire freely and thus give the fleas rheumatism — a hideously unpleasant complaint for an insect which has to jump for its life every few seconds.

[GBS *enters*.]

GBS: It is St Patrick's day and I am in Damascus. I ask myself whether I shall persuade Sister Laurentia to get a hundred days' indulgence, a tailormade short skirt, gaiter boots, a Fair Isle pullover, a smart waterproof, a field glass and camera, a brown sun umbrella lined with red, and a Revelation suitcase, and hasten hither to see for herself what she has imagined at Stanbrook. I leave that question unanswered; but I will tell you what might happen to you because it has happened to me. You would enter the Holy Land at night, with strange new constellations all over the sky and the old ones all topsy turvy, but with the stars soft and large and down quite close overhead in a sky which you feel to be of a deep and lovely blue. When the light comes you have left the land of Egypt with its endlessly flat Delta utterly behind, and are in a hilly country, with patches of cultivation wrested from the omnipresent stones. The appearance of a woman with an infant in her arms takes on the quality of a vision. On this first hour you do not improve. It gives you the feeling that here Christ lived and grew up, and that here Mary bore him and reared him, and that there is no land on earth quite like it. Later on, the guides try to be more exact. This, they tell us, is the stable in the inn. This is the carpenter's shop. This is the upper chamber where the Last Supper was served. You know that they are romancing — there is not a scrap of evidence. In Nazareth you know that Mary used the well in the street because there was (and is) no other well in the town to use; but the water she drew is gone, and the new water, with taps affixed by the British mandatory Government, is anybody's and everybody's water. Everything else in Nazareth, except its natural beauty as a hill town, is a fraud, meanly commemorated by an unattractive and unimpressive church. Because one muddy bend of the Jordan is labelled as the spot on which the dove descended, the whole river is desecrated to make trade for the stall that sells the mud in bottles. I swam in the lake of Tiberias with a pleasant sense that this, at least, was Christ's lake on which nobody could stake out the track on which he walked or the site from which the miraculous draught of fishes was hauled. It is better to have Christ everywhere than somewhere, especially somewhere where he probably wasn't. The hills rise almost into the mountains over the train to Jerusalem, which winds between them so sinuously that you can see its tail from the window. When you arrive you are surprised: the place has a flourishing modern suburban air. The church of the Holy Sepulchre, to eyes accustomed to western architecture of the same period, is a second rate affair; and the squabbles of the sects over their "rights" in it are not edifying. I duly squeezed myself into the sepulchre, and tipped the queerly robed priest who touched my hands with oil, looking as credulous as I could so as not to hurt his feelings; but my thought was that you would be disappointed.

[GBS *leans on his walking stick, wearily mopping his brow.*]

For the rest of the day I damned Jerusalem up hill and down dale; and when they took me to the Mount of Olives (practically oliveless) and showed me the famous view of the city, my only comment was, "Just like Buxton". But one's appreciation is more complex than that. When you stand on the stone from which the Ascension took place you feel at the same moment everything that the legend means you to feel and a purely comic amusement at the notion of Jesus going up to the highest attainable points as a taking-off place for his celestial flight. Your faith and your tourist's observation jostle one another in the queerest fashion.

DLM: Dear Brother Bernard, You have made me feel that I have seen the Holy Land through your eyes, and have revealed a great deal more than I should have seen with my own. I have therefore decided not to procure the attractive outfit you describe, and to continue to view the world from my cell at Stanbrook. I am not at all troubled to think that the most sacred spots in the Holy Land cannot be identified; quite the contrary. It would hurt much more if Christ were, so to say, localised in Palestine — if there were a Christian Mecca. "The earth is the Lord's" and He is everywhere spiritually and most truly accessible. Yet to be in the Holy Land, whatever the drawbacks, and see with your bodily eyes the landscape that Our Lord saw, and swim in his lake, must be a very blessed thing; and I am thrilled by being allowed to share your experience so fully.

[SCC *puts aside the catalogue he is compiling; exhausted, he removes his spectacles and wipes his eyes.*]

SCC: I have been hopelessly pressed and busy: a visit to St James's Palace to see the pictures, a meeting of the Art Workers' Guild, lunch with Dr James at Eton and on to Taplow to spend the night with Walter de la Mare and his family in their charming new home; to a meeting of the Society of Antiquaries to hear a paper on English medieval manuscripts; with Charlotte Mew to a lecture on Shakespeare by Granville Barker; to another lecture by Flinders Petrie on last winter's discoveries in Egypt (old Lady Lytton was my companion and a very nice one she proved); to the Royal Society's *conversazione*; to Brother Bernard's *Caesar and Cleopatra*; tea with this person, dinner with that. You will see that it is a hard life, a tortured existence, and that nothing ever gets done — though I did manage to buy a superb 13th century Nôtre Dame Bible; it is quite magnificent and in remarkably good condition. I wish you could mount your broomstick and come to see it.

DLM: What a whirl you live in! When do you get time to *think*? The Nôtre Dame Bible sounds splendid. I really must look up the condition of my broomstick.

GBS: Dear Sister Laurentia, You asked me for a relic from Calvary — but Calvary is only a spot on a church pavement, jealously guarded, and with nothing removable about it. Where the real Calvary is nobody knows; for the hills outside the city are innumerable. The alleged Via Dolorosa I traversed in a motor car hooting furiously at the children to get out of the way. So off I went to Bethlehem; and from the threshold of the Church of the Nativity, I picked up a little stone, a scrap of limestone rock which certainly existed when the feet of Jesus pattered about on it and the feet of Mary pursued him to keep him in order. In fact I picked up two little stones: one to be thrown blindfold among the others in Stanbrook garden so that there may always be a stone from Bethlehem there, though nobody will know which it is and be tempted to steal it, and the other for your own self. You shall have them when I return, unless I perish on the way, in which case I shall present myself at the heavenly gate with a stone in each hand, and St Peter will stand at attention and salute the stone (incidentally saluting ME) when he has unlocked the gate and flung it open before me. At least he would if it were ever locked which I don't believe.

[DLM *picks up a small silver reliquary and shows it to* SCC.]

DLM: Brother Bernard gave us this. Isn't it beautiful?

SCC: Very, very beautiful.

DLM: It's so generous of him. We all feel quite overwhelmed. It's a reliquary, do you see? — for the little stone he brought back from Bethlehem.

SCC: It looks almost medieval.

DLM: Yes, doesn't it? I'm amazed there are silversmiths who can still do this sort of work.

SCC: There's no inscription.

DLM: Should there be?

SCC: Well, it might be a good idea: a brief inscription explaining its purpose and saying who it's from.

DLM: Yes, perhaps.

SCC: Wouldn't that be a good idea?

DLM: Perhaps we should ask Brother Bernard what he thinks.

GBS: Dear Sister Laurentia, Cockerell is a heathen atheist: a reliquary is no more to him than a football cup. What the devil — saving your cloth — could we put on it? We couldn't put our names on it — could we? That seems to me perfectly awful. "An inscription explaining its purpose!" If we could explain its purpose we could explain the universe. I couldn't. Could you? If Cockerell thinks he can — and he's quite capable of it — let him try, and submit the result to the Pope. Dear Sister: our fingerprints are on it, and Heaven knows whose footprints may be on the stone. Isn't that enough?

DLM: Dear Brother Bernard, I want to tell you how much the beautiful reliquary is admired and appreciated by Lady Abbess and all the nuns.

> [*She starts packing apples in a box.*]

You know by making such a gift to a place like this you expose yourself to the danger of being prayed for very earnestly. I hope you won't be like the man who retorted, when someone promised to pray for him, that he would have none of those underhand ways. You have placed us all in your debt and you must take the consequences.

GBS: I don't mind being prayed for. When I tinker with my wireless set I realise that all the sounds in the world are in my room; for I catch them as I alter the wave length receiver — German, French, Italian and unknown tongues. The ether is full of prayers too; and I suppose if I were God I could tune in to them all. Nobody can tell what influence these prayers have. If the ether is full of impulses of goodwill to me so much the better for me; it would be shockingly unscientific to doubt it. So let the sisters give me all the prayers they can spare; and don't forget me in yours.

DLM: Dear Mr Cockerell, This is chiefly to notify you that a hamper of apples will be sent to you within the next few days. We are simply overwhelmed with apples, and are spending our time gathering and consuming them.

SCC: [*there is a bowl of apples on his table*] The magnificent apples arrived this morning amidst much rejoicing. They must surely be the finest apples since the Garden of Eden, and they have given me a fellow feeling for Adam that I never had before. I have seen nothing of Brother Bernard lately and I suppose he is electioneering for the Labour party. I shall be voting Tory. I am afraid of Labour's rashness, though all my sympathies were once in that direction.

[DLM *is still polishing and packing apples.*]

I finish up with my love and an ardent desire to see your face as soon as I can get to Worcester. P.S. Thank you again for the super apples. I hope you are well.

DLM: I am so glad the hamper arrived safely. I am notorious for my predilection for apples, and should certainly behave no better than Eve in the same circumstances. [*bites into an apple*] I am very well, thank you, and quite jolly, as I have every reason to be.

[SCC *takes a knife and starts to peel one of the apples circularly, in one unbroken strip.*]

SCC: I was a passionate collector from the cradle; I collected mosses, butterflies and moths, all sorts of insects, shells, fossils, stamps — everything. And then it was books: books, fine printing and old manuscripts. As a young man I worked with William Morris at the Kelmscott Press; and later, when he died . . .

[*The apple peeling now completed,* SCC *cuts the apple into quarters.*]

. . . I made use of my natural instinct for collecting to help a number of wealthy connoisseurs acquire rare and ancient manuscripts. [*eats the first quarter of apple*] Among these collectors was my friend, Dyson Perrins — Perrins of Lea and Perrins, the Worcester Sauce people. On the Eve of Epiphany, 1907, we went to Stanbrook to examine a 13th century English Psalter.

DLM: I remember hearing Mr Perrins's car snorting under my window and wondering who and what had come to disturb the peace.

SCC: The Stanbrook Abbey Press was founded in the 1870's. Its purpose was to supply the needs of the house and of the English Benedictine monks and nuns; and also from time to time to publish works of sound spiritual or intellectual value. My interest in their community was sharpened by the fact that Ruskin once told me that he had it in his mind to write a life of St Benedict, but I don't think he ever got very far with it. I was deeply impressed by Dame Laurentia's scholarship; and the faces of the nuns showed me that they were serenely happy, though removed from so much of the world and its wonders. [*eats another quarter of apple*] My first visit to Stanbrook set me thinking a good deal.

DLM: What am I to say about the sources of what you are pleased to call my "scholarship"! St Benedict's daughters have a traditional love of study, though they like to keep quiet and hidden. The little knowledge I possess has been gained in the course of my "religious life", as we call it.

[GBS *listens with increasing interest.*]

We are, for instance, very interested in the movement for restoring the original Plainsong, and since we use the medieval version daily in choir, we have studied the matter pretty thoroughly. You are quite right in believing that we are intensely happy. For my own part I believe no one on earth should be so happy as a nun. Our monastic life is a world in itself, full of wonders of its own, full of reality, and full of interest. Of course all such happiness presupposes a call to the life. ·

[GBS *speaks to* DLM.]

GBS: Tell me how you spend your days. I've no idea what you do.

DLM: What do you imagine?

GBS: I imagine . . . well, I imagine many hours of prayer. Music. The choir in your chapel. Simple meals. Contemplation. Walks in the garden. Quietude. Tranquillity.

DLM: [*smiles*] There's rather more to it than that; our life is very full.

[SCC, *filling his hot-water bottle from a kettle, listens.*]
We rise at 5.00; Lauds is at 5.30; at 6.00, there's half-an-hour of prayer, and then the knock is given for sung Prime; then early Mass, and then at 7.45, breakfast — a cup of tea, which we drink standing up; then there's an hour of manual labour: cleaning our cells, the dormitories and the church (that's frightful if you're not used to it; you get terrible housemaid's knee!). Solemn Mass is at 9.00, preceded by Terce, or Terce and Sext, or Terce, Sext and None; at 10.15 we read from the scriptures; then there's an hour of study; dinner is at 11.30, then an hour of recreation; at 1.30 we have our work to do — and that might be sewing, embroidery, or working at the looms (we make all our own habits) — there's fruit gathering, lavender gathering, the cows and chickens to be fed — and the two pigs (Gog and Magog). Our printing work keeps us busy, too: translating, scribing, and many other jobs; the Stanbrook Press is very demanding. This is where Mr Cockerell has been so wonderfully helpful; he's lent us specimens of fine printing, guided us, taught us, and given us the greatest possible encouragement. His knowledge in the field of books and art is remarkable — unique and truly inspiring. We owe him a very great deal. At 2.45 there's tea; 3.00 o'clock, Vespers; 3.30, conference in the Chapter House; 4.30, study, reading, prayer, and at 6.00 o'clock, supper; then there's recreation — a stroll in the garden, perhaps; at 7.30, Compline, at 8.30, Matins, and then we go to bed — usually about 10.00 or 10.30. It's the same every day; 365 days a year; no holidays, no days off.

[GBS *stares at her.*]

GBS: I am truly amazed; exhausted by the mere thought of it. Did you always intend to lead this sort of life?

DLM: No, no, by no means. I came here to school, you see; in those days I was a nun-hater and was quite certain I should never want to be one. But then, at Christmas, my father wrote to me; "Are you happy?" he asked. I chewed my pen, examined the question from every angle, wanted to say I was miserable, but had to tell him the truth; so I took up my pen and wrote quickly, "Yes, I am very happy." That question of his persisted; I considered it more deeply than I had ever considered anything before. Then I realised that Our Lord was asking for my heart. I could not keep it from Him.

[Birdsong and distant chant.]

SCC: My brief visit to Stanbrook yesterday was quite perfect. What a treat to see you! The lovely singing will never quite die out of my heart. As I was driving home I saw hares playing in the fields and the plovers and larks overhead, and I thought of you and I was sorry that you are cut off from the thrill it all gave me. May I not be sorry that you miss these things?

DLM: Do not think of us as being caged; we do not answer a bit to that description.

[Plainchant has faded.]

Inside the walls of our own paradise we have enough living creatures to satisfy even St Francis. Hares are scarce, but we have delightful rabbits; and as to birds, our larks and nightingales are unequalled, and the thrushes here sing as they sing nowhere else, not even in Scotland. The only place where there is any impression of cutting off is the parlour, and we look on the grille as a barrier, not to keep us in but to keep you out.

SCC: I admit that we are all caged in some way, and that you are free from some of the shackles that bind other women. And as to keeping *me* out, I accept that situation cheerily and if you like you may say that it is I that am imprisoned on the wide earth. I love the fight, such easy part as I take in it, and would not be behind a grille, sheltered from the thorns and thistles, for anything.

DLM: You do not think — do you? — that in religious life one avoids thorns and thistles. Communities often undergo severe trials of one sort or another. To begin with, eighty-four people cannot live together without occasional sparks being struck out. I often think it's the greatest miracle: to have all these nuns living together — day in, day out — and not to have had a single murder yet!

SCC: You ask me whether I think that in the religious life the thorns and thistles are avoided — I do indeed think so. In a community of women, renouncing the world's vanities and all vowed to the same celestial service, I cannot see that there is more opportunity for serious transgression than in a prison. Of course I know that your splendid sympathies enable you to roam in the spirit far beyond your Abbey walls, and almost to share some of the wounds received by your friends, though not to share their risks.

DLM: I don't wish to make you believe that we are the most deeply afflicted people on earth! — only to remark that one does not get out of troubles by leaving the world.

SCC: I can see that the life that you chose when so young has been full of blessings; but if you were to have that choice again, would you repeat it?

DLM: Yes, most certainly I would.

[GBS *is listening to this debate.*]

I sometimes marvel at my wisdom in making the choice, for I was young and fairly foolish and terribly fond of pleasure. Perhaps my youth had something to do with the wisdom I displayed, for I think the young often have a clearness of vision as to the right thing for them. A vocation — any kind of vocation — is a very personal matter, with a subtle and almost irresistible force, and its effects are very enduring. It is *une affaire du coeur*, if you like to call it so, for one's heart cannot rest in earthly things if the call is heard.

SCC: Like you, I would ask no better than to repeat my life, mistakes, follies, and all, knowing how much more than my proper share of good fortune I have had. And as for temptations, I am thankful to have had them, even though I may sometimes have fallen. Walter de la Mare was here on Thursday and I was discussing these things with him. We agreed that the game called Life was infinitely interesting and the more one saw of men and women, if only as passers in the street, the better.

DLM: You are right, of course, in saying that we are all caged; the question is — what kind of people are the most free or the least caged? The answer will depend on what we understand by freedom.

> [SCC *ponders this challenge; meanwhile,* GBS *is putting on outdoor clothes; as he speaks, he searches for — and eventually finds — a pair of shears, and rehearses some sharp cutting movements.*]

GBS: I have never struggled. I was and am incapable of struggling. My incapacity amounts to imbecility. Things have not happened to me; on the contrary, it is I who have happened to them; and all my happenings have taken the form of books and plays. I could write; and I wrote every day. I can remember no time at which a page of print was not intelligible to me, and can only suppose that I was born literate. When I was first in company with Anatole France, he asked me who I was. "I am," I replied, "like you, a man of genius." This was, according to his French code, so immodest that it startled him into riposting with, "Ah well: a whore has the right to call herself a pleasure merchant." I was not offended; for it is true that all artists make their livings as pleasure merchants and not as seers and philosophers. As to struggling towards fame or even towards daily bread for the household, a South American sloth would have shamed me. Besides, I dread success. To have succeeded is to have finished one's business on earth, like the male spider, who is killed by the female at the moment he has succeeded in his courtship. I like a state of continual becoming, with a goal in front and not behind. Then, too, I like fighting successful people; attacking them; rousing them; trying their mettle; kicking down their sand castles so as to make them build stone ones. It develops one's muscles. And you learn from it. A man never tells you anything until you contradict him.

> [GBS *walks off briskly to prune his trees.*]

SCC: A few months after my first visit to Stanbrook, I suddenly
       arranged to marry Miss Kingsford. Kate. She was then
       twenty-nine: a talented artist, with an especial gift for
       illuminated manuscripts. Some of her work was very fine
       and gave me the greatest pleasure. I bought her an emerald
       engagement ring, having first received a written undertak-
       ing from the jeweller that he would buy it back at any time
       if in good condition. She is penniless, which to me is rather
       an advantage than otherwise, as I shall be able to treat her
       with the ferocity which is so large a part of my nature. It is
       no rash act. In all *essentials* I think we are in complete
       accordance.

DLM: I simply can't tell you how pleased I am, for I did not like
       the idea of your going through life alone. The complexity
       of married life ought to be very good for your soul — if you
       take it in the proper spirit.

SCC: Kate's friends and relations are naturally a little uneasy at
       her falling prey to an eccentric book collector, but I hope to
       show them that their misgivings are unjustified — *my*
       friends, on the other hand, think *me* a lucky fellow, as no
       doubt I am. I put all the proper arguments before her, and
       quoted what you had said about the awful time my wife was
       likely to have, but she persisted in accepting me — so it's
       not my fault, is it?

DLM: I congratulate you most heartily and wish you and Miss
       Kingsford every blessing and happiness. I wonder if this is
       the answer to one's prayers for you. I hope so. (Though it
       does put a stop to your ever becoming a monk!)

              [DLM *exits.*]

SCC: Poor old Ouida wrote to me from her cottage in Tuscany.
       Her response was characteristically forthright: "I am very
       sorry to hear the news you give me," she said. "Your
       golden hair will soon turn gray. You have such a charming
       life and are so welcome everywhere, that it is really suicide.
       No woman, were she the loveliest of living creatures, is
       worth the sacrifice of a man's life." These words of warn-
       ing had a grain of substance in them. I never understood

my wife; and her illness created many problems for us both. When she was forty-four, only nine years after we were married, she developed disseminated sclerosis and was confined to bed. The rest of her life was clouded by increasing helplessness and pain. We had three children: two girls and a boy: Christopher.

[GBS *enters.*]

GBS: What news from Stanbrook? Have you heard from Sister Laurentia?

SCC: Only a brief line about the election.

GBS: What election?

SCC: Hasn't she told you? The Lady Abbess died last week and there's to be an election on the 24th. I assumed she'd written to you as well.

GBS: No, not a word. How dare she! I feel quite jealous.

SCC: Well, I'm sure she's been extremely busy.

GBS: I wonder what it's like: an election at Stanbrook.

SCC: All very solemn, I gather. They vote in the church, behind locked doors.

GBS: Perhaps they indulge in some form of ecclesiastical elec-tioneering. Do you suppose they do? Banners, perhaps. Perhaps they hoist up their skirts and run around the Abbey carrying banners. "Vote for Sister Sulpicia and short prayers!"

SCC: "Sister Ann stands for cutlets on Friday and breakfast in bed three times a week!"

GBS: "Vote for Dame Laurentia: the enclosed nun with an unenclosed mind!"

[*They both laugh.*]

[DLM *steps forward as if addressing the nuns at Stan-brook; she is wearing the Abbess's cross and ring.*]

DLM: This is the first time I have the right to address you, my dear Sisters, and my first word is of thanks, not for the honour, though it is a great honour to be an Abbess of Stanbrook, but for your confidence. And to your generous confidence, I can very easily, without a great act of faith, make a return in kind, and I want to say at once that I have the deepest confidence in the Community as a whole and in each member. We could not have a better foundation to start on. True confidence includes mutual frankness, and this, I hope, will be our aim. A bishop said when elected, "I have heard the truth for the last time," meaning that henceforth he would be flattered or perhaps only half-informed. There should be nothing of that between us; the Abbess should be able to hear freely and to speak freely. So we begin with trust in God and each other. To do what? Kind people writing to us hope that we may go from strength to strength — please God we shall, but it will only be by putting the first things first. Any good that will come out of this house will be the fruit of the spiritual life that is led by each.

SCC: Very dear Sister, That you would be elected Abbess seemed a certainty. I congratulate the Convent with all my heart on having at its head one of the wisest and best of women.

DLM: My dear Friend, Thank you for your good letter. It is a wonderful thing to be, spiritually, the mother of eighty souls — a very ennobling responsibility, for we have a great inheritance and a great tradition to uphold.

GBS: I am sure that your election will be no more than a nominal change; for you would boss the establishment if you were only the scullery maid; and now that you are Abbess I feel comforted because you won't have to wash dishes as well as boss; and I wish you a wilful dominating interfering managing sort of Prioress so that you may henceforth have as little to do as possible except keep people's souls clean, as you help to keep that of your erring and worldly Brother Bernard.

SCC: A friend came to supper last evening and entertained us with this story: a rich lady died in Egypt and her nephew, after ascertaining that her will was satisfactory, cabled to have the body embalmed and sent to England for burial.

The coffin arrived in due time, but when they unscrewed it they were dismayed to find that it contained the remains not of the aunt but of a Russian general, who had died and had been embalmed at the same time. They telegraphed to Russia to ask that the mistake should be rectified and got back the answer: "Your aunt buried with full military honours; do what you please with the General"!

DLM: What a capital story about the embalmed aunt! It reminds me of one Cardinal Gasquet told us after one of his visits to America. A certain man's mother-in-law went to Denver for her health and there died. A telegram was sent to the son-in-law: "Mother-in-law dead. Shall we embalm, cremate or bury?" The answer came, "Embalm, cremate *and* bury — take no risks."

[SCC *laughs, then yawns, drifting slowly into a doze.*]

GBS: Dear Sister Laurentia, As you know, Charlotte and I were in Africa recently. One day we were driving in a car which was unfamiliar to me. Instead of pressing the brake, my foot found the accelerator. In my confusion I turned left and not right; the car went out of control, leaping a bank and careering into the veldt. I braked violently. My wife was thrown forward. The luggage fell on top of her. She was badly knocked about and consequently we were forced to stay in Knysna for several weeks while she recovered. During that time, I wrote a little book which I think might interest you. It is about a black girl converted by a missionary, who takes her conversion very seriously and demands where she is to find God. "Seek and ye shall find Him" is the only direction she gets; so off she goes through the forest, a knobkerrie in her hand. Her search is only too successful. She finds the god of Abraham and the god of Job; and I regret to say that she disposes of them both with her knobkerrie. She meets Ecclesiastes the Preacher, who thinks that death reduces life to futility and warns her not to be righteous overmuch. She meets Pavlov, who assures her that there is no God, and that life is only a series of reflexes. She meets St Peter and St John, who is clamouring in despair for the promised Second Coming, as he cannot die until it happens and he is dreadfully tired of waiting in so wicked a world. Then she finds your friend, whom people call the Conjurer, because they won't listen to his preaching but like his miracles. With a motion of his hand, he produces a cup out of thin air: "Take this and drink in remembrance of me." He gives her his commandment, love one another; but this is not enough for her, as there are people whom she hates and knows she ought to hate; and as to loving people, even if it were always possible, she considers it a great liberty to take with them, and doesn't want everybody to take that liberty with her. A little later, she finds the Conjurer stretched on a cross, acting as a model to an image carver who pays him sixpence an hour, this being the only way in which he can earn his scanty bread. He is talking to an Arab — Mahomet. The Conjurer complains that although people buy any number of wooden images of him on the cross, when he preaches they stone him. Mahomet says he doesn't suffer in that way because although he is also a preacher, and the servant of Allah the just and merciful, he is careful to kill all those who do not believe. He proposes adding the black girl to his already large collection of wives, but only involves himself in a vigorous feminist argument of which he gets the worst. The girl goes off, declaring that when men start talking about women they are unbearable. Finally she comes to a villa with a garden, which a frightfully intelligent-looking but wizened old gentleman is cultivating in a rather amateurish way. On hearing of her quest, he remonstrates with her for her audacity, and confesses that if someone told him that God was coming to pay him a visit he would hide in the nearest mouse-hole. "Besides," he says, "you need not trouble to hunt for God: he is always at your elbow." This impresses the girl so much that she goes into the garden and helps the old gentleman to cultivate it until he dies and bequeaths it to her. Shall I send you the story or not? It is very irreverent and iconoclastic; but I don't think *you* will find it fundamentally irreligious. Perhaps I shouldn't disturb the peace of Stanbrook with my turbulent spirit; but as I want you to go on praying for me, I must in common honesty let you know what you are praying for.

[SCC *begins to stir as* DLM *speaks.*]

DLM: Although I agree with many of your ideas, I could never have forgiven you if you had published that book. However, I'm sure you are going to be good and I feel light and springy again and proud of my dear Brother Bernard. You shall have more prayers by way of reward!

[SCC *wakens abruptly.*]

SCC: I fell asleep and dreamt of my mother. She was a wonderful woman: very pretty and very witty. William Morris was quite bowled over the first time he met her. But she was always something of an invalid — just before her wedding she fell off her horse and had to be married lying down. She had six children and was left a widow when she was thirty-two. My father was a partner in a firm of coal merchants, and we lived at Beckenham, near the Crystal Palace. When he died we moved to the seaside, to Margate, where we became friendly with a Mrs Jesse, who was Lord Tennyson's sister. Her husband was a sea captain, and I remember him telling me, "Marriage should be for five, ten or thirty years, not a permanent arrangement."

[GBS *brandishes a newly-published copy of* The Adventures of the Black Girl in her Search for God.]

GBS: Dear Sister Laurentia, This black girl has broken out in spite of everything. I am sending you an inscribed copy of the first edition. You must forgive its superficial levity. Why should the devil have all the fun as well as all the good tunes? I am afraid to present myself at Stanbrook.

DLM: The fact is our points of view are so different, that talking, or writing, round the subject can be of little use. The only way to comfort me would be for you to withdraw *The Black Girl* from circulation. I think you cannot realise how deeply you have outraged the feelings of those who, like myself, believe in God and Our Lord's divinity. These things are

not vital to you, but they are to millions, and there are
things too sacred to be played with. If you had written
against my father or mother, you would not expect to be
forgiven or received until you had made amends. I implore
you to suppress the book and retract its blasphemies, and
so undo some of the mischief it has wrought. You know
how I value your friendship and how truly I have believed
in you. Is this precious thing to be sacrificed to a book that
is unworthy of you?

GBS: Sister Laurentia, You are the most unreasonable woman I
ever knew. You want me to go out and collect 100,000
copies of *The Black Girl*, which have all been read and the
mischief, if any, done. You think you are a better Catholic
than I; but my view of the Bible is the view of the Fathers
of the Church; and yours is that of a Belfast Protestant, to
whom the Bible is a fetish and religion entirely irrational.
Laurentia: has it ever occurred to you that I might possibly
have a more exalted notion of divinity? You think you
believe that God did not know what he was about when he
inspired me to write *The Black Girl*. What happened was
this: when my wife was ill in Africa, God came to see me
and said, "These women at Stanbrook plague me night
and day with their prayers for you. What are you good for,
anyhow?" So I said I could write a bit but was good for
nothing else. Then God said, "Take your pen and write
what I shall put into your silly head." When I had done so,
I told you about it and you were not pleased at all. So I
went to God and said, "The Abbess is displeased." And
God said, "I am God; and I will not be trampled on by any
Abbess that ever walked." "Well," I said, "she is an obstin-
ate woman who will never let me take her out in my car;
and there is no use your going to have a talk with her; for
you might as well talk to the wall unless you let her have
everything all her own way just as they taught it to her
when she was a child." So I leave you to settle it with God
and his son as best you can; but you must go on praying for
me, however surprising the result may be.

SCC: She did not reply. Shaw's travels sometimes took him past the gates of Stanbrook Abbey, but he never stopped, never went in to make his peace. Friendship flags if one does not keep it warm, and theirs seemed to be at an end. Over a year later, he received through the post a small buff-coloured card. Inside was a simple inscription: "In Memory of September 6th., 1884–1934. Dame Laurentia McLachlan, Abbess of Stanbrook.

GBS: To the Ladies of Stanbrook Abbey, Worcester. Dear Sisters, Through some mislaying of my letters, I have only just received the news of the death of Dame Laurentia McLachlan. I was in Malvern from the end of July until the 16th of September; and I never passed through Stanbrook without a really heartfelt pang because I might not call and see her as of old. But I had no knowledge of the state of her health and no suspicion that I should never see her again in this world. There was a time when I was in such grace with her that she asked you all to pray for me; and I valued your prayers quite sincerely. But we never know how our prayers will be answered; and their effect on me was that I wrote a little book which, to my grief, shocked Dame Laurentia so deeply that I did not dare show my face at the Abbey until I was forgiven. She has, I am sure, forgiven me now; but I wish she could tell me so. In the outside world from which you have escaped it is necessary to shock people violently to make them think seriously about religion; and my ways were too rough. But that was how I was inspired. I have no right to your prayers; but if I should perhaps be remembered occasionally by those of you who recall my old visits I should be none the worse for them, and very grateful. Faithfully, G. Bernard Shaw.

END OF ACT ONE

ACT TWO

SCC is alone, finishing his tea-time boiled egg.

SCC: I first set eyes on GBS in 1886. He was lecturing at Hammersmith. Fairly good, I thought, but nothing wonderful. I met him three years later and we have been friends ever since. Although he is a great and wise man, vociferously acclaimed and applauded the world over, Shaw is not above committing the occasional howler — indeed, his letter to the nuns at Stanbrook could, I suppose, be classed as a super howler. But as he himself once said: "The man who has never made a mistake will never make anything."

[GBS *enters, reading the letter from Stanbrook.*]

He wrote the letter on October 3rd; a reply came by return of post.

[DLM *enters swiftly.*]

DLM: My dear Brother Bernard, As you see, I am not dead. I have only been keeping a Golden Jubilee in the habit, as we express it, and that little card was a souvenir of the event. At such a time my mind recalled old friends, you among them. When next you are in the neighbourhood you must come and see me again. You have my daily prayers. I hope they will have nothing but good results in the future.

GBS: Laurentia! Alive!! Well!!!!! Is this a way to trifle with a man's most sacred feelings? I cannot express myself. I renounce all the beliefs I have left. I thought you were in heaven, happy and blessed. And you were only laughing at me. It is your revenge for that Black Girl. Oh, Laurentia, Laurentia, Laurentia, how *could* you. I weep tears of blood. Poor Brother Bernard.

SCC: Queen Mary came to Cambridge and paid a visit to the Fitzwilliam; it was my privilege as Director of the Museum to show her round and I found her very affable and appreciative, though she speaks with a German accent. I am proud of my work at the Fitzwilliam. When I took up my appointment, the arrangement was utterly barbarous: good and bad pictures, all schools and countries mixed, were packed together on the walls to a ridiculous height. My predecessor was Dr James — now Provost of Eton; and although he had an enormous knowledge of medieval Latin, he had absolutely *no* taste whatever (you had only to look at his house to see that), and he hadn't the *least* idea how to run a museum. He just looked in occasionally to see if there were any letters. I found it a pigsty and turned it into a palace. This did not make me fearfully popular in Cambridge, because I was determined to get my own way. The main problem was money: we needed to raise large sums of money — a task I accomplished with considerable skill. My secret was very simple: never admit the possibility of a refusal. I would select my man — somebody with a lot of money and no children — and get myself invited to dinner with him. Then, over the wine, I would say, "What's going to happen to your collection when you die?" or "What will you do for your old University?" They hardly ever refused to help me. I was told that Queen Mary continually dwelt on the beauties of the Fitzwilliam during the drive back to London. I think I could have made a friend of her if I had gone to Buckingham Palace and written my name in the book. She would have asked me to tea.

[The song of a blackbird.]

DLM: Dear Sydney, It was a great pleasure to have your Easter greetings for one likes to feel one's best friend near at that beautiful time. For us here it is a bit of heaven, and everything was in tune this year, the Community well and vigorous, the weather lovely, myriads of daffodils, violets and primroses, and the birds beyond praising. I am having my annual rapture at the return of spring. It begins on the first morning that I am awakened by a bird's song. This year a blackbird has taken upon itself the office of calling me, and it makes me feel fresh at once. Thrushes used to be my favourite song-birds, but I am now fonder of the blackbird, at least I think I am.

SCC: [*opening a letter and propping a photograph on the mantelpiece*] Dear Sister, Thank you for the photograph; I get much pleasure from your smile on my mantelpiece. It is astonishing to realise that it is twenty-five years since first I saw your face! The impression was bound to be abiding, but I little guessed that I was on the threshold of so long and precious and intimate a friendship. I reckon that first meeting, and always shall, as one of the great events in a not uneventful life. You have given me help and sympathy of a kind that no one else can give. I thank you with all my heart for being the dear and noble lady that you are, and I pray you continue to bear with my defects and my caprices, yourself ever the same, until death do us part.

DLM: Dear Sydney, What a gift and what a mystery our friendship is! It is one of those blessings that seem never to have had a beginning and which one feels are a part of one's very life. I suppose it was just waiting till we were ready for it. May it grow always into still deeper understanding until we are done with this earthly life, and may we come to perfect comprehension in eternal life, where I firmly believe all that is best in us will have its fulfilment. Do say Amen.

> [GBS *puts a record on a wind-up gramophone and then glides gracefully across the stage, executing a complicated sequence of tango steps; he speaks to* DLM. SCC *observes.*]

GBS: The position and carriage of the dancer's head is extremely important. It should be kept erect, with the chin slightly tilted upwards. You should never glance down at your feet. [*still dancing*] The gentleman rests his weight on the right foot — brings his left foot forward for 'one' — swings it behind for 'two' — transfers his weight to the left foot — carries his right foot behind the left for 'three' — brings ths right foot in front of the left for 'four'. This is the third figure of the tango: the *Media Luna.*

DLM: [*smiles*] I'm very impressed.

GBS: And so you should be. I learnt it when I was on holiday in Madeira. The man who taught me was an authority on the tango, which he believes owes its origin to the war dances of ancient Thebes.

       [DLM *laughs;* GBS *continues dancing.*]

       Dance every day for at least a quarter of an hour, and you will become as slim and agile as myself.

DLM: [*another smile*] I think the nuns would be rather alarmed if I did.

       [GBS *stops dancing and turns off the gramophone; he goes to* DLM. SCC *resumes sorting some papers.*]

GBS: Something else happened in Madeira. I meant to tell you. Quite forgot. [*sits to regain his breath*] I met an American. Intelligent, educated, rather charming. Somehow — I've forgotten the circumstances — your name came into the conversation. He was tremendously impressed that I knew you. It seems that his passion in life is plainsong, Gregorian chant; and your book — what is it? — *The Grammar of Plainsong* — is that right?

DLM: Yes.

GBS: Well, clearly he regards it as the most remarkable book ever written on the subject. He said that people come from all over the world to consult you. I had no idea that you were such an expert.

DLM: It is my life's work. I believe that God the Creator made the world for his own glory; and in becoming man He gathered into Himself the whole creation and gave it the voice of praise. We are a small part of that voice. Of course it's no easy task to be at one's best seven times in the day and once in the night; but a chantress *never* stops singing.

SCC: Much amused by a story of Sargent, the portrait painter. He is said to have had a screen in his studio behind which he retired at intervals to put out his tongue at his opulent sitters and shake his fist at them. Having relieved his feelings in that way, he emerged smiling and no one was a penny the worse. By the way, we have a new maid. Her name is Mayzod Tryphena Wesley. Why does that please me so much?

GBS: Dear Sister Laurentia, You cannot imagine how delighted I was to find you shining in all your old radiance. If ever I write an opera libretto, it will be rather like *Die Zauberflöte*; but I shall call it *The Merry Abbess*. As I drove back here it was a magically lovely evening, or seemed so to me. I felt ever so much the better for your blessing. There are some people who, like Judas Iscariot, have to be damned as a matter of heavenly business; and it is clear that I may be one of them; but if I try to sneak into paradise behind you, they will be too glad to see you to notice me.

> [GBS *picks up a newspaper and starts to read; he lowers the paper to listen to* DLM.]

DLM: Where you go eventually depends entirely on you, and you would be wise to choose Heaven. People are not sent to Hell, they go there because they choose that fate. When people talk of going there, it is sometimes a way of giving themselves leave to do as they like, just as when Catholics say they have lost their faith and it nearly always means they have lost their morals. Anyhow, *you* are not going to the wrong place if I can do anything to prevent it!

> [GBS *returns to his newspaper.*]

SCC: I have heard the most astonishing rumour about Mrs Shaw, whom I know very well — or thought I did. It seems that she took a violent fancy to T. E. Lawrence and that they exchanged a number of frank and revealing letters. I find this almost impossible to believe — and since it was I who introduced Lawrence to the Shaws, I also find it rather disturbing. How unpredictable is human behaviour! I remember Thomas Hardy — when he was 84½ years old — falling violently in love with a girl who was acting in an amateur production of one of his plays. For a time he was completely infatuated with her. Mind you, Mrs Hardy (the second Mrs Hardy) was dull beyond description: an inferior woman with a suburban mind — so perhaps it was

not entirely surprising. And even I — who could never be
described as a ladies' man — even I have not escaped the
grip of these troublesome emotions. There was one par-
ticular afternoon. A young woman came to see me. I had
promised to show her some of my books. It was in the
twenties: '23 or '24. In those days, a curtain divided my
study from the room where Kate lay, ill and crippled. I
could hear her moaning with pain. An agonising sound.
She called out, "Sydney, *when* is the nurse coming back?"
"Not long now," I said. Suddenly, and without thinking, I
seized my young visitor and kissed her fiercely on the lips.
She said nothing. She left the house without saying a word.
I was reminded of what Thomas Hardy had told me one
evening: "One of the first rules for a writer of fiction is that
it must not be made so strange as fact."

> [GBS *puts down his newspaper, but uses it as he speaks
> to punctuate his ideas.*]

GBS: The Coronation of King George VI prompts me to revive a
proposal of mine that has never met with any public sup-
port: that is, to institute a Society for the Prevention of
Cruelty to Royal Personages. Of all the instruments of
torture employed the Coronation would be the worst if it
were not so seldom employed. The *Times*, which is expected to say something polite about it, calls it "Tradition
consecrated by a thousand years." The lapse of time does
not consecrate a tradition: it makes an anachronism of it.
The thing has become so absurd that from every quarter
we are urgently reminded that the proceedings are symbolic, and that the King himself is a symbol. But in the
Coronation the symbols are not merely obsolete: they sym-
bolise conditions which have been reversed. They repre-
sent the King's investment with powers that he no longer
wields and of which it has cost us two revolutions and
several regicides to deprive him. The clothes used are the
clothes of William the Conqueror and his Queen, trans-
mogrified by generations of costumiers into fancy dresses
symbolic of nothing but the Russian ballet. If I were in the
royal succession, I would renounce fifty monarchies sooner

than go through such a ritual. I should not be at all surprised to learn that Edward VIII had flatly refused to endure its thousand-year-old tomfooleries, and that this and not his diplomatic masterstroke of marrying an American lady was the real cause of his abdication.

> [GBS *plunges the newsaper, a Coronation edition, into the wastepaper basket; he picks up his hat and walking stick, and exits.*]

SCC: Very dear Sister, The other day, in tidying my table, I came across a letter which I thought might interest you. [*holds the letter in his hand*] It was from Henry Luxmoore, a valiant spirit with very high ideals, who was, for many years, a master at Eton. He told me about his younger brother — a soldier, dear to all — who lay dumb with blood poisoning, throat and mouth most distressful — at the last he sat up in bed, said joyful and clear, "What! Father and mother!" as if in welcome, and died. Luxmoore, deeply moved by this event, asked, "Does that mean *nothing?*"

DLM: The incident related by Mr Luxmoore is very touching and to me simply confirmatory of faith in the immortality of man's soul.

SCC: According to my stony judgement, it does not confirm anything. [*puts Luxmoore's letter into a file*] This short and transitory life seems to me of such small account that I cannot imagine its being a basis for eternity, or for any continuance which would not be as remote from our terrestrial existence as that of a butterfly's from a caterpillar's. And as for the prospect held out, would not most people prefer *not* to meet again the friends and relations they have grown out of?

DLM: Surely one conceives of the future life as being on an entirely different plane from our existence here, — and since the conditions will be so different I think we shall find no inconvenience in meeting even those whom we have outgrown.

SCC: The point is this: you take your creed on trust, asking only the authority and direction of the Church. That creed contains a series of tenets which my reason refuses to accept.

DLM: It's true that we take our creed on the authority of the Church, but we are not asked to abdicate our reason.

SCC: What about God the Father, God the Son, and God the Holy Ghost: how are these 'Persons' to be thought of? Do not the majority of the faithful conceive of them as magnified human beings? Is this not patently impossible? If it be impossible, why does not the Church declare it to be so? And what then becomes of all the beautiful literature of thrones, crowns and the rest, all the anthropomorphic visions on which we have been nourished?

DLM: The pictures of thrones and crowns and the descriptions of visions are symbols adapted to our understanding, and I am sure you are not the man to quarrel with symbols, nor with mysteries.

SCC: I once asked Archbishop Lang how he envisaged God — as a being with arms and legs? "Indeed no," he said. Then I asked why he spoke of God as 'he' instead of 'it', and he said 'it' would never do: 'it' would take away all sense of personal relationship. I suppose he's right; all the same, 'it' seems a lot more honest to me.

DLM: [*switching on a table lamp: a pool of light*] Why is faith difficult in divine things when it is acceptable in human affairs? We believe lots of things in the natural order that we cannot understand. No one knows what electricity is, yet we know something of its power, and use it in a thousand ways.

SCC: [*dusk in his room: an owl hoots*] As far as I am concerned, one is left with great overwhelming mysteries — and no religion (so far as I can see) makes these problems easier of solution. For people of my sort of mind and imagination (both sadly limited) the only honest attitude is that of admitted ignorance. What I may become in future years, if I live, I cannot tell, but I find myself as sceptical and unyielding as ever, and if I change this attitude I think it will be because of wandering powers and interests.

[*It is even darker now around* SCC.]

DLM: There are very few of the problems that vex the minds of men like you, in fact there are probably none, that have not been faced and probably solved by the great minds of Christianity, such as St Augustine and St Thomas Aquinas. I heard not long ago of a young man, not a Catholic, who had been through all philosophies, and who then coming on St Thomas found he filled up all the weak places in the other systems. But you would not read this kind of thing, so you will not give faith a chance.

SCC: You know I read next to nothing outside my work, never find time for reading, being hopelessly lazy when I am not at my desk.

[SCC *switches on his table lamp.*]

[*The sound of an air-raid warning as* GBS *enters, with a torch. He pulls black-out curtains across the window, then switches on a lamp. Thus there are now three pools of light in the darkness.*]

GBS: I am in straitened circumstances to the extent of being overdrawn by several thousands to meet the war taxation; for the success of the *Pygmalion* film, instead of enriching me beyond the dreams of avarice, ruined me by putting me into the millionaire class, which is taxed nineteen and sixpence in the £. To get ten guineas I have to earn £420, which makes me think twice about sums that I could afford to throw about before the war. Charlotte is badly crippled — suffering from the effect of an accident in her teens, and incurable because the only treatment — steel corset, plaster jacket, immobilization for months — is bearable by men under forty only. No danger to her life beyond that of all octogenarians; but she will be an invalid as far as medical science goes: a sentence of lumbago for life.

[*The sound of aircraft overhead.*]

We are very difficult of access here; there is no public conveyance of any kind in the village; and petrol is rationed. The War Office wants to publish three of my plays to prevent them from going mad. I have given them *carte blanche* and the use of my type free, *gratis*, and for nothing. I am damnably old; but as well as can be expected. I can still write a bit.

[*The aircraft sound is louder.*]

DLM: In this lovely September it is difficult to believe that a hideous war is in progress, though we have aircraft over us all day. What a welter the world is in! And how horrible it is to see every man's hand against his brother.

SCC: These devastating air-raids have made me extremely anxious about my precious books and manuscripts. Thankfully, Siegfried Sassoon has offered to give them refuge in his country house, Heytesbury. A great weight off my mind. Kate is safe also, staying with friends in Gloucestershire.

GBS: If I were an Omnipotent Creator I could stop the war in a week by letting loose a few billion locusts and white ants in every acre of territory in the countries of the belligerents. Next day they would be fighting, not each other, but countless numbers of tiny creatures advancing on them with indomitable discipline. There would be no Semites and anti-Semites then, no British and no Germans, no Americans and Japanese, blacks and whites, yellows and reds, no Irishmen even, nothing but men and women fighting frantically for human life.

[*The sound of an explosion.* GBS *sits staring out in his pool of light.*]

SCC: Another of my windows has been smashed at Kew, as well as the conservatory. Every post brings news of some friend whose house has suffered. The longer the nights get the more time there will be for the bombing. After dark it is next to impossible to stop them. Yesterday I lunched with Brother Bernard. We looked at your photograph together and you may have felt your ears burning. His admiration for you is undiminished. I urged him to write and say so. He has got a bit older in the last year, but he was full of a gentle vivacity. Thank you for the sprig of lavender; I carry it in my pocket diary. [*puts the lavender in his wallet*] My love to you, now and always.

DLM: Dearest Sydney, Many thanks for your letter and the message from Brother Bernard, which pleased me very much. He has not written, but I am glad to know that he still keeps a warm place for me in his big heart. It must be rather pathetic to see him growing old and feeble, but there will be a special charm in his gentleness. The hop-picking is going on busily and the air is full of the fumes of dried hops.

> [SCC *picks up the* Times, *reads the obituaries, sees that of Charlotte Shaw, and lowers the newspaper.*]

My love to you, Kate, and the family.

GBS: Mr Bernard Shaw has received such a prodigious mass of letters on the occasion of his wife's death that, though he has read and values them all, any attempt to acknowledge them individually is beyond his powers. He therefore begs his friends and hers to be content with this omnibus reply, and to assure them that a very happy ending to a long life has left him awaiting his own in perfect serenity.

SCC: [*putting down his newspaper*] William Morris was the first person I saw dead. Lady Burne-Jones called me into the room, I remember, and I stood by the bed sobbing uncontrollably as I gazed down at the corpse. I was startled to see how little it resembled the living Morris. The face was singularly beautiful, but the repose of it made it the more unlike what I had known in life. Ruskin once called him "beaten gold". Morris had two daughters, May and Jenny. Jenny was an invalid, suffering from epilepsy from about her sixteenth year. Her sister, May, had many fine qualities, but she was plagued by a gnawing discontent all her life. She always wanted something out of her reach: if she got the moon, she wanted the sun. She married a rather second-rate Socialist named Sparling. She was in love with Bernard Shaw before he was famous, and he with her. Shaw said that "a Mystical Betrothal was written in heaven," but that on earth his poverty prevented their marriage. Stanley Baldwin fell in love with her too, so did Burne-Jones. There was a time when I was rather in love with her myself. Poor May. I saw her into her coffin.

[*Full daylight now.* GBS *is putting on outdoor clothes, going off to post letters.*]

GBS: Dear Sister Laurentia, I hope this will not arrive late for your Diamond Jubilee tomorrow. It is too late for mine by twenty years. You ask me how I am. I must reply, the better for your prayers; for, deaf and doddering and dotty as I inevitably am at my age, I am astonishingly well, much weller than I was a year ago. You would still know me if you met me. I wish you could. I count my days at Stanbrook among my happiest.

[GBS *is about to exit, but is arrested by what* DLM *says.*]

DLM: My dear Brother Bernard, Sixty years of enclosed life leaves me happier than ever for having chosen this path — though as Tagore said: "We cannot choose the best. The Best chooses us." If people only knew the freedom of the enclosed nun! I believe you can understand it better than most people and I only wish we shared the faith that is its foundation. I never forget you in my prayers nor fail to commend you to Our Lady. Your lovely reliquary with its stone from Bethlehem is treasured. Again my best thanks, Sister Laurentia.

[GBS *exits with his letters.*]

SCC: Dearest Sister, Sunday will be the twenty-second anniversary of our blessed and never-to-be-forgotten romp in London. I must write to you today to make sure that my letter of thankfulness for that great occasion be not too late. I can remember it all so clearly, every detail. Most particularly I remember that joyful morning — September 7th., 1922 — when I received your letter telling me that such a treat might be possible.

[*Possibly, in their excitement,* SCC *and* DLM *read parts of each other's letters, he speaking a few of her phrases and vice versa.*]

DLM: Dear Mr Cockerell, I am altogether plainsongy at present, and I have been invited to the Abbey of East Bergholt, Suffolk, to give the nuns a month's choir training. They want me to go now or in the Spring. Now is impossible, for many reasons, and the Spring may be so, but there is a chance of a trip coming off then. Please do not mention this to anyone. You are the only person who I am telling.

SCC: I am much excited by your letter. Can I not meet you at Paddington and pilot you across London *via the British Museum*? It is half way to Liverpool Street!

DLM: How nice of you to be so keen about my news. If the thing comes off I shall do my very best to realise your alluring suggestion about the British Museum, but I have no idea whether London will be allowed. When, and if, the time comes you will have to write to Lady Abbess using all your eloquence, and explaining how the détour could be worked out. How kind of you to think of sending me a hot-water bottle. I am most grateful.

SCC: You must let me know as soon as the dates are fixed. I refuse to admit the possibility of the falling through of this plan!

DLM: Dear Mr Cockerell, I am now able to announce to you that I shall most probably be going to East Bergholt on June 11th. There are still some formalities to be completed, for leave from Rome is required for the expedition, but I think these will be settled in time.

SCC: I am keeping June 11th free so that I may meet you at Paddington. What I should like to be told is: (one) exactly how much time you will have at your disposal for sight-seeing and (two) whether you would like to bestow the whole time with the British Museum or whether you would like to go to the National Gallery as well, or to Westminster Abbey, or etc., etc. Having received this information from you am I to write to the Lady Abbess to get the programme endorsed? Are you just an ordinary mortal on your way through London? — i.e., can you lunch in a public restaurant or must some more holy and secluded place be found?

DLM: My train is due at Paddington at 11.15 and I leave Liverpool Street at 5.42, so that gives us a good day. I should
     like to give all the time possible to the B.M. Lady Abbess
     endorses all this so you need not write to her at present. It
     seems wonderful that I should be making such plans as if
     they were the most natural thing in the world for me to do.

SCC: What fun to have you in London! We shall have such a
     feast of buildings and manuscripts as will make you keep
     the broomstick always in readiness for other visits.

DLM: Dear Mr Cockerell, Lady Abbess woke up this morning
     with an entirely new, and improved, set of ideas about the
     journey. I was very keen on hearing Mass at Westminster
     Cathedral, but it seemed impossible, unless I stayed out a
     night, and that she did not want. However the question is
     solved. I shall go up by an earlier train, reaching Paddington at 9.50, and then I will go straight to the Cathedral for
     10.30 Mass. Could you meet me there and show me
     something of the Abbey before midday? And then go on to
     the B.M.? Or would this be very troublesome for you? Do
     be frank.

SCC: I shall be delighted to fall in with your plans. I will meet
     you at the Cathedral and will arrange about the B.M. It will
     be a very busy day.

DLM: I look forward eagerly to Monday. It will be a delight to see
     you again.

SCC: She heard High Mass in Westminster Cathedral.

DLM: Then we went to see the view of London from Westminster Bridge.

SCC: In the afternoon she was shown privately, under the best
     official guidance, some of the principal manuscript treasures of the British Museum.

DLM: The Lindisfarne Gospels, Queen Mary's Psalter and the
     Lambeth Bible.

SCC: We left at 4.40 and motored to Liverpool Street Station.

DLM: Dear Mr Cockerell, What is to be said about yesterday? It
     was a day of perfect joy to mind and heart and will ever live

as a golden memory. I thank God for every moment of it and I thank you for your very large share in making it happy. It was all so unexpected (though not undreamed of) that I felt in a way rapt with its wonderfulness and meaning, and at the same time it all seemed perfectly natural and right. Those hours in the B.M. were pure bliss. But there is no good saying more. You understand, and know how much I appreciate all you did and your way of doing it.

SCC: Yes, it was indeed the reddest of red-letter days, and I am already beginning to doubt whether it was all true, just as I doubted beforehand whether it was ever going to happen. You must have been dead tired when we said goodbye to you. I rejoice that you have seen and handled those glorious manuscripts, and I am proud to have been present when they were set before you. It was a hasty feast, but of the very best. Quite seriously, it was one of those great days of my life that I expect to recall on my deathbed, if I have a deathbed and not the sudden ending that I wish for my friends and for myself.

> [GBS *enters, wearing an eye-shade and carrying secateurs. Birdsong from the garden. A feeling of autumn and bonfires.*]

GBS: I have requested that no inscription on any monument to me shall imply that I belonged to any established religious denomination, and that the monument itself shall not take the form of a cross, or any other instrument of torture. As to Westminster Abbey, I have no fancy for it; my ghost would be bored by big buildings.

> [DLM *is reading the* Times.]

I need seasons: trees and birds. What I should really like would be a beautifully designed urn on a little pedestal in the garden here, with Charlotte and myself inside listening for the first cuckoo and the nightingale and scenting the big cherry tree.

DLM: Dear Brother Bernard, If I had forgotten, the announcement of "GBS 90" would have reminded me that your perennity is about to reach the pleasant age of four-score and ten.

[GBS *takes off his gardening gloves and eye-shade.*]

You will be bothered with so many letters that I will only say: God bless you, and may you go on and on in the track of Methuselah.

[GBS *puts on some black slippers, rests his feet on a stool, takes a boiled sweet from a jar, and leafs through a bundle of telegrams.*]

GBS: I had a word with Cockerell on the birthday. He is beginning to look a bit oldish; but he can walk without a stick, which I dare not attempt, as the police would charge me with being drunk and incapable. However, I am quite happy in my garden, where the weeks race past like minutes; their speed is incredible. One day I must sit down and do a little radical pruning before it's too late — pruning of myself, I mean; I need pruning, there's a lot of dead wood. I wrote about music, I wrote about art, I wrote about the theatre, I wrote novels, I wrote plays, I preached at the City Temple, I professed atheism, I was a funny man, I was a dangerous man, I was an agitator, I was a Fabian, a vegetarian, and now I'm a millionaire. All unconnected and uncollected odds and ends. It's time the masks were burnt; I've had enough of them. It is time I became an individual.

[SCC *is examining a Sotheby's catalogue, checking the books that are to go to the next sale.*]

SCC: As well as acquiring rare books and manuscripts for connoisseurs and the Fitzwilliam, I have, over the years, managed to build a not inconsiderable library of my own. Neither poverty nor the responsibilities of marriage could curb my collector's instinct. It was never any use my swearing to stop buying things; the moment I was sufficiently tempted I always fell! Fortunately, I started collecting when booksellers weren't educated — when they couldn't read Latin. Thus many of my manuscripts are now worth ten times what I paid for them; often substantially more. An English tenth-century Boethius, which I bought in 1909 for £75 is now worth £6,600; and the Six Dialogues of Plato, which cost £24 in 1920, is now valued by

Sotheby's at £5,800. Of course these sums of money aren't important in themselves; but it's nice to know that I can now afford to have an egg with my tea.

[SCC *puts the books into a neat pile; he energetically sips tea.*]

GBS: [*it is night time; September*] Dear Sister Laurentia, A few weeks ago I had a visit from another very special friend whose vocation was as widely different from yours as any two vocations on earth can be, and yet who is connected in my thoughts with your subject, the efficacy of prayer. He is Gene Tunney, an Irish American, still famous as the un-defeated Heavy Weight Boxing Champion of the World, no less. He is a good man all through, and entirely present-able in any society. He comes of a devout Catholic family, pillars of The Church; but, as he puts it, "When I went into the ring as a professional I dropped all that." But though he dropped the faith it did not drop him. He made a fortune by his fights and when he retired he married a rich woman. The young couple came travelling to Europe, and found themselves on a pleasure island in the Adriatic, when I met him and made friends with him. He told me what had just happened to him. His young wife was attack-ed by a very rare complaint, unknown to most surgeons, of a double appendicitis. Nothing but a major operation could save her; and there was on the island only one old and useless doctor. Death within ten hours was certain. Gene, helpless and desperate, could only watch her die. Except one thing, to go back to his faith and pray. He prayed. Next morning very early there landed on the island the most skilful surgeon in Germany, the discoverer of double appendices. Before ten o'clock Mrs Tunney was out of danger and is now the healthy mother of four children. Protestants and sceptics generally see nothing in this but a coincidence; but even one coincidence is improbable, and a bundle of them as in this case hardly credible in a world full of miracles. The prayer, the timing of the surgeon's arrival, his specialisation for the rare disease, were so complicatedly coincidental that if they had been reported

to me from China about strangers I should not have believed the story. As it is I do not doubt it; and it goes to
confirm the value I instinctively set on your prayers. So do
not forget me in them. I cannot explain how or why I am
the better for them; but I like them and am certainly not
the worse. Perhaps I have told you the Tunney story
before; old men tend to repeat their stories mercilessly. No
matter; it will bear twice telling. [*checks his pocket watch*] I
am so very old (ninety-two) that you would hardly know me
if I could now get as far as Stanbrook. I am very groggy on
my legs, and make blunders by the dozen; but although my
body is going to bits, I have passed the second childhood
that comes at eighty or thereabouts and got that clear
second wind that follows it. My soul still marches on. Do
not for a moment feel bound to answer this; you have no
time for duty letters. A hail on my next birthday, if it ever
arrives, will satisfy me.

[*The three friends are very close here.*]

SCC: Dearest Sister, Kate had a slight stroke last month; she lost
ground, became unconscious, and this morning, to my
great relief, the end came. I am very thankful that her life
was not further prolonged; I think it has been a happy one
on the whole, in spite of more than thirty years of disabling
illness. I am also thankful that I did not go first, as it would
have made things very difficult for her.

DLM: Dearest Sydney, There is no need to say how truly I
sympathise with you and the family. I am with you in
thought and prayer.

SCC: A long time ago, when the children were small, Kate wrote
to me a short but heartfelt letter. What event or incident
prompted her to do so, I have quite forgotten. "It often
grieves me very much," she said, "that you don't try to see
more of the children, because if you don't make intimate
friends of them now you will never be able to, and it will
make you awfully unhappy when they are bigger when you
will want to help them and won't be able to get near them."
Dear Kate. She was a remarkable and courageous woman.

The funeral was very simple. I took some of her books to the Mortlake Crematorium: the five books she wrote as well as illustrated. We looked at these in turn for half-an-hour and then came home. I went to bed early feeling thankful that a difficult day had passed off so satisfactorily. [*indicates a bookcase*] I keep her ashes there: in that casket on the bookcase, so that one day they may be mingled with my own.

> [DLM *is sitting in a wheelchair, now severely incapacitated, able only to move her neck and hands. She is reading the* Times *and singing abstractedly to herself: a phrase of Gilbert and Sullivan.*]

DLM: "I am the monarch of the sea,

The ruler of the Queen's Navee,

Whose praise Great Britain loudly chants:

And we are his sisters and his cousins and his aunts."

> [*In the middle of the last line the Abbey clock strikes and simultaneously a bell rings for Compline.* DLM *looks up at the crucifix on her wall, and starts to pray silently. As if prompted by some form of telepathic communication,* SCC *hums the last few bars of the Gilbert and Sullivan.*]

> [GBS *sits amidst a litter of manuscripts, discarded wrapping paper and unopened letters.*]

GBS: Dearest Sister Laurentia, I got your letter on my birthday: the only one that was not hurried into an overloaded waste paper basket with very unseemly objurgations. So many people in Ireland kept sending me parcels of food and little presents that I had no use for, and that many of them could ill afford, that I had to declare publicly that I needed nothing that money could buy, and asked only for their unpurchasable prayers. Since then I have been so overwhelmed with prayers that I am in danger of my Eternal Judge exclaiming "Damn this fellow that I am being pestered about: to hell with him." I get piles of medals of the Blessed Virgin, with instructions that if I say a novena she will give me any help I ask from her; and I have to reply that we are in this wicked world to help her and not to beg from her. For some inexplicable reason I put Stanbrook prayers into a class by themselves, and have no fear of their getting on heavenly nerves. All my worldly goods are vanishing into the till of Sir Stafford Cripps. I had to sell all my books and furniture in London, and clear out into a cheaper furnished flat at the same address.

> [GBS *switches on the radio, listening to Verdi's Requiem:* Libera me.]

I am horribly old (ninety-three) and cannot walk much. Happily my wits are livelier than my legs; but I cannot in the course of nature last much longer. Cockerell and I correspond quite often. Do not dream of having to answer this: it is only to let you know that the thought of Stanbrook is a delight to me. It is one of my holy places.

DLM: My dear Brother Bernard, The lavender harvest has just come in and one of my jobs is to pack it in to little bags for our sale of work.

> [GBS *falls asleep.*]

You will accept it as thanks for the very kind and unexpected letter you wrote me, and I hope the fragrance will keep you in mind of Stanbrook, where you are so affectionately remembered. There is a little medal of Our Lady in the lavender, but you will not object to that. The prayers go on.

> [GBS *is motionless; a bag of lavender falls from his hand. The Verdi continues, very distantly.*]

SCC: GBS died on November 2nd., 1950. I think I was his oldest living friend; and although I miss him very much, I was thankful to hear that the end had come, as he was eager for it in his last uneasy days. I had a deep esteem for him. He had all the attributes of a gentleman — unswerving integrity, consideration for others, generosity on the sly. I went to Golders Green for the cremation: the first time I had been on a train for nine months. There was no religious ceremony. The organist played one of Elgar's Enigma Variations and *Libera me* from Verdi's Requiem, in accordance with a wish expressed by Shaw to Lady Astor. Between these performances I read (very badly) the final words of Mr Valiant-for-Truth from *The Pilgrim's Progress*, a book greatly admired by GBS all his life, with the passage ending "and all the trumpets sounded for him on the other side." I think nothing could be more appropriate for the occasion.

DLM: Dear Brother Bernard has indeed been fitly honoured. I shall always be grateful to you for the friendship of this great and dear man. His fidelity to that friendship was always a marvel to me. I grew fonder of him year by year. Dying on All Souls' Day he will have the prayers of many.

GBS: We have to face the fact that we are a very poor lot. Yet we must be the best that God can as yet do, else he would have done something better. I thing there is a great deal in the old pious remark about our being worms. Modern science shows that life began in a small, feeble, curious, blind sort of way as a speck of protoplasm; that, owing to some sort of will in this, some curious driving power, always making for higher organisms, gradually that little thing, constantly trying, and wanting, having the purpose in itself, being itself a product of that purpose, has by mere force of wanting and striving to be something higher gradually, curiously, miraculously, continually evolved a series of beings each of which evolved something higher than itself. And what is to be the end of it all? There need be no end. There is no reason why the process should ever stop, since it has proceeded so far. But it must achieve on its infinite way the production of some Being, some Person if you like, who will be strong and wise, with a mind capable of comprehending the whole universe and with powers capable of executing its entire will: in other words, an omnipotent and benevolent God.

[*Lights fade on* GBS.]

SCC: Dearest Sister, I am rather a poor thing with wits and memory in a sad way, but I cannot forget tomorrow's anniversary of our trip to London twenty-nine years ago.

To think of it! We have now been friends for more than half our lives! What a strange and lucky chance brought us together, and how easily I might never have known you! And then I should never have surmised how great had been my loss. I have been in bed all this year with heart trouble — a little discomfort but no pain to speak of; and I have lots of very nice visitors and do not repine. But I feel spent and good for nothing. If I could go off quickly like the King I should be glad, as my work is finished. How are you, my dear? I hope you can give me a far better account of yourself. I send you my special love and infinite thanks for all you have been and meant to me.

DLM: Dearest Sydney, This unforgettable date brings the very happiest memories and I wish I could explain how much our day at the British Museum enriched my mind and heart; and how it left me happier than ever in my life and full of amazement at the way in which the promised hundredfold is bestowed. I go over every detail of that day with joy and gratitude to you: from the drive through the poppy-lined lanes of Worcester and the first sight of you at Westminster Cathedral, to our farewells at Liverpool Street station. Of course we have altered a good deal since then, and your note tells me of your disabilities. I cannot visit you as so many other faithful friends do, but my thoughts are often with you, and my prayers.

> [*A moment of pain;* DLM *utters a soft, gasping moan; the spasm passes.*]

I have been rather unwell all this year but I am better again and taking up work gradually, though I am going very *piano*, with plenty of resting, and locomotion is largely in a wheelchair. Thank you for your beautifully-written note. I hope it did not cost you too much. With my love and the happiest remembrance for all the years since we first met in 1907.

SCC: Grievous news from Dame Laurentia. She is dangerously ill with congestion of a lung. This may be the last letter I shall receive from her. It is written in a firm hand. She says that she is holding her own.

DLM: What a mystery friendship is! And how strangely and delightfully different one's friends are one from the other — not only in themselves, but in the way one has to look at them. Some we have to carry, while others carry us. The perfect friend, to my mind, is one who believes in you once and for all, and never requires explanations and assurances. True friendship is one of those subtle and beautiful forces that glorify life.

> [*The Abbey choir can be heard singing* Cum transieris per aquas tecum ero; DLM *listens for a moment and then speaks the text.*]

Cum transieris per aquas tecum ero, et flumina non operient te: When thou shalt pass through the waters, I will be with thee, and the rivers shall not cover thee.

> [*Lights fade on* DLM; *the singing voices also fade.*]

> [*A bell tolls. The garden door is open. The sound of a cuckoo.*]

SCC: A very great lady is dead. In the course of a long life I have known no other woman at once so wise, so learned, so saintly, and so brim-full of kindness and compassion. And now she is dead: beloved and honoured by all who knew her. A card announcing her death ended with these words: "Strengthened by the rites of Holy Church she gave up her soul to God on the 23rd August, 1953, in the 88th year of her age, the 69th of her monastic life and the 22nd of her rule as Abbess."

> [*A moment of silence: then the telephone rings.* SCC *lifts the receiver and bellows into it.*]

Hello, yes? . . . What? . . . Yes, speaking — Cockerell speaking . . . What? Who? . . . You'll have to speak up, I'm extremely deaf . . . What? . . . Yes . . . Who are you? What have you done? . . . What? . . . What books? What exhibition? . . . What? . . . No, it's out of the question, I can't do that . . . What? . . . No, I cannot lend any of my books for your exhibition, I'm sorry. I've sold most of them, anyway . . . No, no, I won't change my mind, there's no possibility of that. I'm expecting to die any moment now, and if I let you have them it would lead to the most dreadful complications . . . Yes, I'm sorry — goodbye. [*hangs up; pause*] Another winter gone and I'm still a prisoner to my room. I expected to be dead by now, but I am content to live on until I become a greater nuisance to those about me. Apart from a slight weakness in the chest, I feel distinctly better than I did a year ago. I attribute this to my doing next to nothing. [*Pause.*] I once thought I was rather a smart young man; I now realise I was only second-rate. I was a born intriguer and puller of strings; and that is how I strove to justify my otherwise useless existence — by bullying those who were more gifted than myself and getting the best out of them. But I've had a very interesting life. Apart from Kate's lamentable illness, I should like to have it all over again. [*Pause.*] The secret of a happy and interesting life is to talk to *everyone, everywhere.* One day, for example, while strolling in Kew Gardens, I made the acquaintance of a nice Indian mathematician from Bangalore, a cultivated German silk merchant who had lived for a long time at Watford, and a burly American surgeon who wanted to see a robin. I enjoy these chance encounters. Most people never take advantage of them. [*Pause.*] Twice last night I woke up with my mind out of control. My thoughts wandered aimlessly. This has happened once or twice before and is very disagreeable — perhaps a touch of madness. [*Pause.*] Spent most of the afternoon reading my diary for 1934 and found it absorbingly interesting. I noted that on the 17th of June of that year I had lived exactly the same time — 33 years and 168 days — in the 19th and 20th centuries. How fascinating is the pattern of one's life! [*Pause.*] Darling Freya Stark came to see me. I am so deaf now that we had to have a *written* conversation. She's a marvellous little woman — a real brick: very small, with a strongly arched nose and a whimsical expression. I'm amazed that she has sufficient stamina for all those exhausting journeys. [*Pause.*] I remember going for a walk with two of my children when they were about six or seven. Margaret asked who made God, and what there was before the world was created. Then Christopher asked whether when we are dead we shall remember being alive. Margaret thought that we might live again as birds. Then she said that after we were dead we should be part of history. Perhaps I shall soon know the answers. [*Pause.*] I had a very bad night of choking and coughing. I thought the end was very near. Alarming symptoms in the afternoon. I had a sudden temperature and did not recognise people, not even the doctor. [*Pause.*] I am a sad coward, terribly afraid of pain. [*Pause.*] I leave my children a number of the best and kindest friends, both men and women, that ever man had. Gratefully conscious of all they have meant to me, I declare friendship to be the most precious thing in life. But it is like a plant that withers if it is not heedfully fostered and tendered. It is only by constant thought, by visits, by little services, and by abounding sympathy at all times, that friends can be kept. I implore my children to remember this, so that the blessings that have been mine may be theirs also. [*Pause.*] A young man came to see me to talk about Ruskin. Described my last meeting with the great man. Said it was like interviewing a ghost. Young man, shy; I stone deaf; so we didn't make much progress. A wasted morning. [*Pause.*] Slept from 9.15 to 5.15; my best night for ever so long, but awoke feeling weak and silly. The Angel of Death seems quite to have forgotten me. On the other hand, I might pop off tomorrow. Who knows?

> [SCC *looks at his watch; records the time in his diary. A cuckoo sings distantly as he winds his watch.*]

SLOW CURTAIN